TO EBERHART FROM GINSBERG

TO EBERHART FROM GINSBERG
A Letter About HOWL 1956

AN EXPLANATION BY ALLEN GINS-
BERG OF HIS PUBLICATION *HOWL*
AND RICHARD EBERHART'S *NEW
YORK TIMES* ARTICLE "WEST COAST
RHYTHMS" TOGETHER WITH COM-
MENTS BY BOTH POETS AND RELIEF
ETCHINGS BY JEROME KAPLAN

THE PENMAEN PRESS 1976

ISBN: 0-915778-09-2 (signed hardcover)
ISBN: 0-915778-08-4 (unsigned softcover)
ISBN: 0-915778-07-6 (unsigned hardcover)

Penmaen Press Books are published by Michael McCurdy at the Penmaen Press, Old Sudbury Road, Lincoln, Massachusetts 01773.

TO EBERHART FROM GINSBERG

How This Book Came Into Being

I SUPPOSE I should make mordant remarks about the folly of being comforted by reviewing the times and events of a poem published twenty years ago. Twenty years is more or less a literary generation and Ginsberg's *Howl* ushered in a new generation. I well remember being in San Francisco and hearing him read it at Ruth Witt-Diamant's house filled with eager listeners of his age-group and some older members like Rexroth and Ferlinghetti. They were all there, all of those remarkable young poets who were soon to make their marks. I regret to mention any name because you know them all. They were soon to be called the Beats. I remember being amazed and delighted way up in the hills to hear Duncan recite with splendid modulation hundreds of lines of Milton at a time. Mike McClure's high-flying imagination eventuates in a new play in San Francisco this fall. Last spring the then-young Snyder won the Pulitzer Prize. All of these poets made a unique contribution to modern American poetry.

The most spectacular poem of the group, a loose-jointed non-federation of individualists, was undoubtedly *Howl*. Ginsberg learned that *The New York Times* had asked me to write a piece about what was happening on the West Coast. I had forgotten, but scholarship helps me now to learn, that Kenneth Rexroth made the suggestion. The article was to come out in the early fall of 1956. One could not have imagined what would happen to any of us in twenty years.

Young Ginsberg, keen and alert, wanted to make sure that I knew what he was up to in writing his long poem and wrote me the long letter published here for the first time. I recall my delight at his meticulous approach to his work, and want to state again the fierce, strident impact this work had on its excited first hearers before it became generally known. Within a short time *Life* magazine published a large spread on these young poets, which gave them national attention. The rest, you might say, has been history of the past twenty years. I recall in that early time hearing the word Kerouac. I thought this a foreign and most odd-sounding word, one which I had never heard before. As years passed it became a household term, not odd-sounding at all.

I felt from the start that Ginsberg had what I call a spiritual quality. I would be hard put to define this term but I felt it strongly about his poetry and I feel it still. It is an aggression upon the unseen to make it seen; a grasp of significance beyond real things being presented in activated, exalted, and original lines; a climate of high imagination and imaginistic force in the weather of the moment. With the perspective of twenty years this first perception is borne out in Ginsberg's subsequent handling and embracement of Indian mysteries and mysticism. I subscribe to the totality of his imagination.

8

The strong social criticism offered by *Howl* left me with admiration for the poem but I must have said to him, I do not remember how or when, that it did not teach me how to live, an attitude he countered. I felt that it was destructive and did not in itself evoke a better life while it showed evils of society of the time. I thought I must have answered the letter here printed, but here scholarship fails me for I cannot find an answer in my archives. I would much like to know what I would have said in rejoinder at the time.

Years passed and every now and then I would get out this letter and read it, or parts of it, to my classes. It always stimulated students, made them think, opened their minds to heady discussions. Sometimes I would read the piece to the students. I recall one time being unable to hear it through, it was so harsh and strident. Then I lost the letter, one year could not find it in my study. Some years passed and I found it, made sure I had a few copies made so as not to lose it again.

The next point in the history of this book is that when Michael McCurdy asked me if I had anything further to propose to his press after *Poems to Poets* I thought of this letter. Ginsberg was contacted and said that he could not remember having written it. Against a loss of the manuscript, and his forgetfulness, by chance we are both able to present this work twenty years later together with "West Coast Rhythms", where in retrospect I was cast in the role of Mercury.

Richard Eberhart
October 25, 1975

More Explanations Twenty Years Later

WHAT I didn't say to Eberhart: *Howl* is really about my mother, in her last year at Pilgrim State Hospital—acceptance of her, later inscribed in *Kaddish* detail.

The campaign of vilification and denigration that the first "Beat" texts met—interpreted from *Partisan Review* thru *Time* and even in FBI files as incomprehensible antisocial wild-eyed hate-filled irrational rebellious protest—was what I was foreseeing and trying to avoid as politely and straightforwardly as possible.

Kerouac sickened and died of the rejection of his tenderest feelings toward America as Corso indicates in *Elegaic Feelings American.*

The element of parody and humor in characterization of certain nutty cases alluded to (Part I *Howl*) has been missed, even by members of a later generation schooled in Acid madness and tolerance of temporary tripping-out and temporary beatitude—and misinterpreted as "anger." Yes there's plenty of anger and resentment in *Howl*, but distanced by eternal perspective and comic sympathy sufficient to make balanced protest of compassion. The word protest, properly used, means pro-attestation, that is testimony in favor of Value (not a resentful cry against the national universe). Thus *Howl* seems to be a "protest poem," tho the word's been much abused by left and right politicos and journalists.

Some prophetical insights are clearer now—such as the phrase "scholars of war"—referring to a class of intellectuals who made fortunes refining their aggressions, and projecting them internationally, as Cold War Thinkers —social scientists "thinking the unthinkable" to show they were smarter harder-headed than the Military, their unsympathetic machismo bankrupting these States— historians apologizing for Indochinese & Middle East Hot Wars, scientists inventing Napalm and Plutonium with the alibi of "pure scientific research" as in Burroughsian fiction, Secretaries of State from Dulles to Kissinger rationalizing aggressive military gang-warfare suitable to their oil-company employers, CIA sponsored editors promoting hard-line essays on Realpolitik in international mental magazine networks—all these madmen were later struck down by post-Watergate drunken taxicabs of Absolute Reality.

At the time I believed in some sort of God and thus Angels, and religiousness—at present as Buddhist I see an awakened emptiness (Sunyata) as the crucial term. No God, no Self, not even great Whitman's universal Self, it's still Self, as God would be. The defect in these poems & this letter to Richard Eberhart is the insistence on a divine self rather than a relatively heavenly emptiness. But it was implicit that mindfulness insight and perfection of Self would lead to no-Self.

I was writing to Eberhart with point of reference to the experience of vast space displayed in last lines of his great *Groundhog* poem—which I associated with my own "mystical" experience of an Endless Present catalysed by a few poems of Blake six years previous.

I've grown more and more to respect W.C. Williams' "mad rules—indefinable tho they be at present" for his short line verses & his "relative measure" triadic verse-lines. The elements of judgement used to determine exactitudes in these modes can be named and taught—1) attention to raw matter of common speech & local diction 2) eye-page artistic balance 3) breath stop and speech-mind hesitancy 4) run-on lines counter to breath-stop, and breath-stop counter to run-on enthusiasms, for purpose of syncopation or subtlety of pronunciation 5) surprise balances, to emphasize ideas, phrases, or even conjunctions and articles, 6) measurement of relative weight of ideas from phrase isolated on page, or relative weight and importance of different phrasings 7) inner-ear awareness of stress, quantity, assonance rhyme and offrhyme etc. embedded in separated fragments of speech being balanced together 8) logical analysis or break-down of sentence-mind-think-wave, beginning at left hand margin and spread along page till thought finishes toward right hand margin—somewhat as grammarians diagram a sentence visually, with drooping dependent clauses and adjectives hanging from nouns 9) conditions of parchment, pocket note-book short-lined & record-ledger long-lined, determining line-length of versification, typewriter mystiques and practicalities, prescription pad condensations and abruptness 10) quirkiness and care-lessness as well as accidents of speech and transcription conscious and valuable 11) count of syllables 12) playful genius Common Sense—These are some of the particular considerations which can make "open" verse forms "Artful". PLACEMENT AND BALANCE OF LINES MUST BE "MINDFUL". This mindfulness as in sitting meditation or tea ceremony, mindfulness of each articulate gesture, is the elemental character of Williams' mode in his own poetry and in his later practitioners' poetics.

The *attempt* to balance the phrasings is in itself the "discipline"—discipline was misinterpreted popularly in the '50's as a set of fixed (generally stressed iambic count) rules rather than an attitude of awareness of problems of contemporary verse-formation and an attempt to make balanced divisions of speech-matter.

Pound's mindfulness was of quantity—length of vowels—and in that he had "a mystical ear"—that was Williams' exquisite praise of Pound.

The reader will find further experiments with the long or strophic line in the poems *Kaddish* and *The Change*.

"Moloch whose name is the Mind!" seems to be the key phrase of the poem—rhythmically it is the climax of that rhapsody.

Allen Ginsberg
October 6, 1975

A Letter to Eberhart

ALLEN GINSBERG

Dear Mr Eberhart:

Kenneth Rexroth tells me you are writing an article on S.F poetry and asked for a copy of my MSS. I'll send it.

It occurred to me with alarm how really horrible generalizations might be if they are off-the-point as in newspapers.

I sat listening sans objection in the car while you told me what you'd said in Berkeley. I was flattered and egotistically hypnotized by the idea of recognition but really didn't agree with your evaluation of my own poetry. Before you say anything in the *Times* let me have my say.

1) The general "problem" is positive and negative "values". "You don't tell me how to live", "you deal with the negative or horrible well but have no positive program" etc.

This is as absurd as it sounds.

It would be impossible to write a powerful emotional poem without a firm grasp on "value" not as an intellectual ideal but as an emotional reality.

You heard or saw *Howl* as a negative howl of protest.

The title notwithstanding, the poem itself is an act of sympathy, not rejection. In it I am leaping *out* of a preconceived notion of social "values", following my own heart's instincts—*allowing* myself to follow my own heart's instincts, overturning any notion of propriety, moral "value", superficial "maturity", Trilling-esque sense of "civilization", and exposing my true feelings—of sympathy and indentification with the rejected, mystical, individual even "mad".

I am saying that what seems "mad" in America is our expression of natural ecstasy (as in Crane, Whitman) which suppressed, finds no social form organization background frame of reference or rapport or validation from the outside and so the "patient" gets confused thinks he is mad and really goes off rocker. I am paying homage to mystical mysteries in the forms in which they actually occur here in the U.S. in our environment.

I have taken a leap of detachment from the Artificial preoccupations and preconceptions of what is acceptable and normal and given my yea to the specific type of madness listed in the Who section.

The leap in the imagination—it is safe to do in a poem.

A leap to actual living sanctity is not impossible, but requires more time for me.

I used to think I was mad to want to be a saint, but now what have I got to fear? People's opinions? Loss of a teaching job? I am living outside this context. I make my own sanctity. How else? Suffering and humility are forced on my otherwise wild ego by lugging baggage in Greyhound.

I started as a fair-haired boy in academic Columbia.

I have discovered a great deal of my own true nature and that individuality which is a value, the only social value that there can be in the Blake-worlds. I see it as a "social value".

I have told you how to live if I have wakened any emotion of compassion and realization of the beauty of souls in America, thru the poem.

What other value could a poem have—now, historically maybe?

I have released and confessed and communicated clearly my true feelings tho it might involve at first a painful leap of exhibition and fear that I would be rejected.

This is a value, an actual fact, not a mental formulation of some second-rate sociological-moral ideal which is meaningless and academic in the poetry of H———, etc.

Howl is the first discovery as far as *communication* of feeling and truth, that I made. It begins with a catalogue sympathetically and *humanely* describing excesses of feeling and idealization.

Moloch is the vision of the mechanical feelingless inhuman world we live in and accept—and the key line finally is "Moloch whom I abandon".

It ends with a litany of active acceptance of the suffering of soul of C. Solomon, saying in effect I am *still* your amigo tho you are in trouble and think yourself in a void, and the final strophe states the terms of the communication.

"oh starry spangled shock of Mercy"

and mercy is a real thing and if that is not a value I don't know what is.

How mercy gets to exist where it comes from perhaps can be seen from the inner evidence and images of the poem —an act of self-realization, self-acceptance and the consequent and inevitable relaxation of protective anxiety and selfhood and the ability to see and love others in themselves as angels without stupid mental self deceiving moral categories selecting *who* it is safe to sympathize with and who is not safe.

See Dostoyevsky and Whitman.

This process is carried to a crystal form in the *Sunflower Sutra* which is a "dramatic" context for these thoughts.

"Unholy battered old thing O sunflower O my soul
I LOVED you then."

The effect is to release self and audience from a false and self-denying self-deprecating image of ourselves which makes us feel like smelly shits and not the angels which we most deeply are.

The vision we have of people and things outside us is obviously (see Freud) a reflection of our relation to our self.

It is perhaps possible to forgive another and love another only after you forgive and love yourself.

This is why Whitman is crucial in development of American psyche. He accepted himself and from that flowed acceptance of all things.

The *Sunflower Sutra* is an emotional release and exposition of this process.

Thus I fail to see why you characterize my work as destructive or negative. Only if you are thinking an outmoded dualistic puritanical academic theory ridden world of values can you fail to see I am talking about *realization* of love. LOVE.

The poems are religious and I meant them to be and the effect on audience is (surprising to me at first) a validation of this. It is like "I give the primeval sign" of Acceptance, as in Whitman.

The second point is technical. This point would be called in question only if you have not Faith. I mean it is beside the true point and irrelevant because the communication, the *sign* of communication if successfully made should begin and end by achieving the perfection of a mystical experience which you know all about.

I am also saying have faith that I am finally referring to the Real Thing and that I am trying to communicate it.

Why must you deny your senses?

But as to technique—[Ruth] Witt-Diamant said you were surprised I exhibited any interest in the "Line" etc.

What seems formless tho effective is really effective thru discovery or realization of rules and meanings of forms and experiments in them.

The "form" of the poem is an experiment. Experiment with uses of the catalogue, the ellipse, the long line, the litany, repetition, etc.

The latter parts of the first section set forth a "formal" esthetic derived in part incidentally from my master who is Cezanne.

The poem is really built like a brick shithouse.

This is the general ground plan—all an accident, organic, but quite symmetrical surprisingly. It grew (part III)

The poem is really built
like a brick shithouse

Section 1 — Catalogue (fixed base w/ ho)

Section 2 — Repetition & variation (fixed base m/ doch)

Section 3 — fixed base / reply / fixed base / longer reply / etc

This is the General Ground
Plan — all an accident, organic
but quite symmetrical surprisingly

out of a desire to build up rhythm using a fixed base to respond to and elongating the response still however containing it within the elastic of one breath or one big streak of thought.

As in all things a reliance on nature and spontaneity (as well as much experience writing and practicing to arrive at spontaneity which IS A CRAFT not a jerk-off mode, a craft in which near-perfection is basic too) has produced organic proportion in this case somewhat symmetrical (i.e. rationally apprehensible) proportion.

This is, however, vague generalization.

The Long Line I use came after 7 yrs. work with fixed iambic rhyme, and 4 yrs. work with Williams' short line free form—which as you must know has its own mad rules —indefinable tho they be at present—

The long line, the prose poem, the spontaneous sketch are XX century French forms which Academic versifiers despite their continental interests (in XIX century French "formal" forms, Baudelaire) have completely ignored. Why?

This form of writing is very popular in S.A. and is after all the most interesting thing happening in France.

Whitman
Apollinaire
Lorca

Are these people credited with no technical sense by fools who by repeating the iambic mouthings of their betters or the quasi-iambic of Eliot or the completely irrational (tho beautiful) myth of "clear lucid form" in Pound—who works basically by ear anyway and there isn't any clear mentally formulizable form in him anyway, no regular countable measure*—I'm straying—people who by repeating etc., are exhibiting no technical sensitivity at all but merely adeptness at using already formulated ideas —and *this* is historically no time for that—or even if it were who cares, I don't. I am interested in discovering what I do *not* know, in myself and in the ways of writing— an old point.

The long line—you need a good ear and an emotional ground-swell and technical and syntactical ease facility and a freedom "esprit" to deal with it and make of it anything significant. And you need something to say, i.e. clear realized feelings. Same as any free verse.

The lines are the result of long thought and experiment as to what unit constitutes *one speech-breath-thought.*

```
I have observed my mind
"      "        "        " speech  1.) Drunk
                                   2.) Drugged
                                   3.) Sober
                                   4.) Sexy etc.
```

---

* An error here, as Pound attempted to approximate classical quantitative measure. (Allen Ginsberg, 1975)

And have exercised it so I can speak *freely*, i.e. without self-conscious inhibited stoppings and censorships which latter factors are what destroy speech and thought rhythm.

We think and speak rhythmically all the time, each phrasing, piece of speech, metrically equivalent to what we have to say emotionally.

Given a mental release which is not mentally blocked, the breath of verbal intercourse will come with excellent rhythm, a rhythm which is perhaps unimprovable.

[Unimprovable as experiment in any case.

Each poem is an experiment

Revised as little as possible.

So (experiments) are many modern canvasses as you know. The sketch is a fine "Form".]

W.C. Williams has been observing speech rhythms for years trying to find a regular "measure"—

he's mistaken I think.

There is no measure which will make one speech the exact length of another, one line the exact length of another.

He has therefore seized on the phrase "relative measure" in his old age.

He is right but has not realized the implications of this in the long line.

Since each wave of speech-thought needs to be measured (we speak and perhaps think in waves)—or what I speak and think I have at any rate in *Howl* reduced to waves of relatively equally heavy weight—and set next to one another they are in a balance O.K.

The technique of writing both prose and poetry, the technical problem of the present day, is the problem of Transcription of the natural flow of the mind, the transcription of the melody of actual thought or speech.

I have leaned more toward capturing the inside-mind-thought rather than the verbalized speech. This distinction I make because most poets see the problem via Wordsworth as getting nearer to actual *speech*, verbal speech.

I have noticed that the unspoken visual-verbal flow inside the mind has great rhythm and have approached the problem of Strophe, Line and stanza and measure by listening and transcribing (to a great extent) the coherent mental flow. Taking *that* for the model for Form as Cezanne took Nature.

This is not surrealism—they made up an artificial literary imitation.

I transcribe from my ordinary thoughts—waiting for extra exciting or mystical moments or near mystical moments to transcribe.

This brings up problems of image, and transcription of mental flow gives helpful knowledge because we think in sort of surrealist (juxtaposed images) or haiku-like form.

A haiku as the 1910–20's imagists did *not* know, consists of 2 visual (or otherwise) images stripped down and juxtaposed—the charge of electricity created by these 2 poles being greater when there is a greater distance between them—as in Yeats' phrase "murderous innocence of the sea"—2 opposite poles reconciled in a flash of recognition.

The mind in its flow creates such fantastic ellipses thus the key phrase of method in *Howl* is "Hydrogen Jukebox" which tho quite senseless makes in context clear sense.

Throughout the poem you will see traces of transcription, at its best see the last line of *Sunflower Sutra*, "mad locomotive riverbank sunset frisco hilly tincan evening sitdown vision".

This is a curious but really quite logical development of Pound-Fenelossa-Chinese Written Character-imagist W.C. Williams' practice.

I don't see the metrics or metaphors as revolution, rather as logical development, given my own interests, experiences, etc. and time.

This (explanation) is all too literary as essentially my purpose has been to say what I actually feel, (not what I want to feel or think I should feel or fit my feelings into a fake "Tradition" which is a *process* really not a fixed set of values and practices anyway—so anybody who wants to hang on to traditional metrics and values will wind up stultified and self-deceived anyway despite all the sincerity in the world). Everybody thinks they should learn academically from "experience" and have their souls put down and destroyed and this has been raised to the status of "value" but to me it seems just the usual old fake death, caused by fear and lack of real experience. I suffered too much under Professor T——, whom I love, but who is a poor mental fanatic after all and not a free soul   I'm straying.

2) *The poetry situation in S.F.*

The last wave was led by Robert Duncan, highly over-literary but basic recognition of the spontaneous free-form experiment. He left for Mallorca and contacted Robert Creeley,editor of *Black Mountain Review*, they came friends and Duncan who dug Williams, Stein, etc. especially the Black Mountain influence of Charles Olson who is the head peer of the East Coast bohemian hipster-authors post Pound. Olson's *Death of Europe* in *Origin* last year (about a suicide German boy)—"oh that the Earth/had to be given/to you/this way." is the first of his poems I've been able to read but it is a great breakthrough of feeling and a great modern poem I think.

Creeley his boy came here [San Francisco] last month and made contact with us—and next issue of *Black Mountain Review* will carry me, Whalen and:

1) William S. Burroughs, a novelist friend of mine in Tangiers. Great Man.
2) Gary Snyder, a Zen Buddhist poet and Chinese Scholar 25 years old who leaves next week for further poetry study in a Zen monastery in Kyoto.
3) Jack Kerouac, who is out here and is the Colossus unknown of U.S. Prose who taught me to write and has written more and better than anybody of my generation that I've ever heard of. Kerouac you may have heard of but any review of the situation here would be ultimately historically meaningless without him since he is *the*

unmistakable fertile prolific Shakespearean *genius*—lives in a shack in Mill Valley with **Gary Snyder.** Cowley (Malcolm) is trying to peddle him in N.Y.C. now* and can give you info. Kerouac invented and initiated my practice of speech-flow prosody.

I recount the above since anything you write will be irrelevant if you don't dig especially Kerouac—no shit, get info from Kenneth [Rexroth] or Louise Bogan who met him if you don't take my word.

The W.S. Burroughs above mentioned was Kerouac's and my mentor 1943–1950.

I have written this in the Greyhound between loading busses and will send it on uncensored.

I've said nothing about the extraordinary influence of Bop music on rhythm and drugs on the observation of rhythm and mental processes—not enough time and out of paper.

Yours Allen Ginsberg

---

* Cowley as editor at Viking was having difficulty persuading the management to publish *On The Road.* (Allen Ginsberg, 1975)

May 18 [1956]
I am off to the Arctic part of Alaska on a USMSTS re-
supply ship for the DEW line radar installation. Mail for
me will be forwarded—A. Ginsberg c/o Phil Whalen, 1624
Milvia Street, Berkeley, Cal. See you next Xmas.

Allen

(*The following pages were appended to Ginsberg's letter*)

Summary

I. VALUES

1) *Howl* is an "affirmation" of individual experience of
   God, sex, drugs, absurdity etc. Part I deals sympathetically with individual cases. Part II describes
   and rejects the Moloch of society which confounds
   and suppresses individual experience and forces the
   individual to consider himself mad if he does not re-
   ject his own deepest senses. Part III is an expression
   of sympathy and identification with C.S. [Carl Solo-
   mon] who is in the madhouse—saying that his madness basically is rebellion against Moloch and I am
   with him, and extending my hand in union. This is an
   affirmative act of mercy and compassion, which are
   the basic emotions of the poem. The criticism of
   society is that "Society" is merciless. The alternative
   is private, individual acts of mercy. The poem is one
   such. It is therefore clearly and consciously built on
   a *liberation* of basic human virtues.

To call it work of nihilistic rebellion would be to mistake it completely. Its force comes from positive "religious" belief and experience. It offers no "constructive" program in sociological terms—no poem could. It does offer a constructive human value—basically the *experience*—of the enlightment of mystical experience—without which no society can long exist.

2) *Supermarket in California* deals with Walt Whitman. Why?

He was the first great American poet to take action in recognizing his individuality, forgiving and accepting *Him Self*, and automatically extending that recognition and acceptance to all—and defining his Democracy as that. He was unique and lonely in his glory—the truth of his feelings—without which no society can long exist. Without this truth there is only the impersonal Moloch and self-hatred of others.

Without self-acceptance there can be no acceptance of other souls.

3) *Sunflower Sutra* is crystallized "dramatic" moment of self-acceptance in modern terms.

"Unholy battered old thing, O sunflower O my soul, I *loved* you then!"

The realization of holy self-love is a rare "affirma-tive" value and cannot fail to have constructive in-fluence in "Telling *you* (R.E.) [Richard Eberhart] how to live."

4) *America* is an unsystematic and rather gay exposition of my own private feelings contrary to the official dogmas, but really rather universal as far as private opinions about what I mention. It says—"I am thus and so I have a right to do so, and I'm saying it out loud for all to hear."

II. TECHNIQUE

A.   These long lines or Strophes as I call them came spontaneously as a result of the kind of feelings I was try-ing to put down, and came as a surprise solution to a met-rical problem that preoccupied me for a decade.

I have considerable experience writing both rhymed iambics and short line Post-W.C.W. [William Carlos Williams] free verse.

Howl's 3 parts consist of 3 different approaches to the use of the long line (longer than Whitman's, more French).

1. Repetition of the fixed base "Who" for a cata-logue.
   A. building up consecutive rhythm from strophe to strophe.

B. abandoning of fixed base "who" in certain lines but carrying weight and rhythm of strophic form continuously forward.

2. Break up of strophe into pieces within the strophe, thus having the strophe become a new usable form of stanza—Repetition of fixed base "Moloch" to provide cement for continuity. *Supermarket* uses strophe stanza and abandons need for fixed base. I was experimenting with the form.

3. Use of a fixed base, "I'm with you in Rockland," with a reply in which the strophe becomes a longer and longer streak of speech, in order to build up a *relatively* equal nonetheless free and variable structure. Each reply strophe is longer than the previous. I have measured by ear and speech-breath, there being no other measure for such a thing. Each strophe consists of a set of phrases that can be spoken in one breath and each carries relatively equal rhetorical weight. Penultimate strophe is an exception and was meant to be—a series of cries—"O skinny legions run outside O starry spangled shock of mercy O victory etc." You will not fail to observe that the cries are all in definite rhythm.

The technical problem raised and partially solved is the break-through begun by Whitman but never carried forward, from both iambic stultification and literary automatism, and unrhythmical short-line verse, which does not yet offer any kind of *base* cyclical flow for the build up of a powerful rhythm. The long line seems for the moment to free speech for emotional expression and give it a measure to work with. I hope to experiment with short-line free verse with what I have learned from exercise in long.

B.   Imagery—is a result of the *kind* of line and the kind of emotions and the kind of speech-and-interior flow-of-the-mind transcription I am doing—the imagery often consists of 1920's W.C.W. [Williams] imagistically observed detail collapsed together by interior associative logic—i.e., "hydrogen jukebox," Apollinaire, Whitman, Lorca. But *not* automatic surrealism. Knowledge of Haiku and ellipse is crucial.

West Coast Rhythms

RICHARD EBERHART

THE West Coast is the liveliest spot in the country in poetry today. It is only here that there is a radical group movement of young poets. San Francisco teems with young poets.

Part of this activity is due to the establishment of the Poetry Center at San Francisco State College three years ago. Its originator and moving spirit is Ruth Witt-Diamant, who began by offering readings by local poets and progressed to importing older poets from the East. She hopes next to stimulate the writing of verse drama.

Part of the activity of the young group has been inspired by Kenneth Rexroth, whose presence in San Francisco over a long period of time, embodying his force and convictions, creates a rallying point of ideas, interest and informal occasions. The influence of Kenneth Patchen is also felt by this group. Robinson Jeffers looms as a timeless figure down the Coast.

Some of the interest may also be attributed to the universities, colleges and schools where an unusual number of poets teach and write. These poets are older than the youngest group, which is still in its twenties.

The second important center of poetry on the West Coast is Seattle, where the University of Washington is notable for its work in poetry. Theodore Roethke has enlivened this region for a number of years. Stanley Kunitz has been there this past year. Nelson Bentley, William H. Matchett and Kenneth Hanson are active young poets there. Carol Hall, Caroline Kaizer and Richard Hugo, not directly connected with the University, are also producing. Melvin LaFollette, a graduate, writes in Vancouver.

In the Bay region there are several poetry readings each week. They may be called at the drop of a hat. A card may read "Celebrated Good Time Poetry Night. Either you go home bugged or completely enlightened. Allen Ginsberg blowing hot; Gary Snyder blowing cool; Philip Whalen puffing the laconic tuba; Mike McClure his hip highnotes; Rexroth on the big brass drum. Small collection for wine and postcards . . . abandon, noise, strange pictures on walls, oriental music, lurid poetry. Extremely serious. Town Hall theatre. One and only final appearance of this apocalypse. Admission free."

HUNDREDS from about 16 to 30 may show up and engage in an enthusiastic, free-wheeling celebration of poetry, an analogue of which was jazz thirty years ago. The audience participates, shouting and stamping, interrupting and applauding. Poetry here has become a tangible social force, moving and unifying its auditors, releasing the energies of the audience through spoken, even shouted verse, in a way at present unique to this region.

The Bay region group, by and large, is anti-university. Its members make a living at odd jobs. Ambiguity is despised, irony is considered weakness, the poem as a system of connotations is thrown out in favor of long-line denotative statements. Explicit cognition is enjoined. Rhyme is outlawed. Whitman is the only god worthy of emulation. These generalizations would probably not be allowed by all members of the group. They may serve, however, as indicators.

The most remarkable poem of the young group, written during the past year, is *Howl*, by Allen Ginsberg, a 29-

year-old poet who is the son of Louis Ginsberg, a poet known to newspaper readers in the East. Ginsberg comes from Brooklyn; he studied at Columbia; after years of apprenticeship to usual forms, he developed his brave new medium. This poem has created a furor of praise or abuse whenever read or heard. It is a powerful work, cutting through to dynamic meaning. Ginsberg thinks he is going forward by going back to the methods of Whitman.

My first reaction was that it is based on destructive violence. It is profoundly Jewish in temper. It is Biblical in its repetitive grammatical build-up. It is a howl against everything in our mechanistic civilization which kills the spirit, assuming that the louder you shout the more likely you are to be heard. It lays bare the nerves of suffering and spiritual struggle. Its positive force and energy come from a redemptive quality of love, although it destructively catalogues evils of our time from physical deprivation to madness.

In other poems, Ginsberg shows a crucial sense of humor. It shows up principally in his poem "America," which has lines "Asia is rising against me./ I haven't got a Chinaman's chance." Humor is also present in "Supermarket in California." His "Sunflower Sutra" is a lyric poem marked by pathos.

Lawrence Ferlinghetti is the publisher of the Pocket Poet Series from his bookshop in San Francisco, the City Lights Pocket Bookshop. Small, inexpensive paper books have already appeared by Rexroth, Patchen, W.C. Williams with Ginsberg, Denise Levertov and Marie Ponsot scheduled to follow. Rexroth's "Thirty Spanish Poems of Love and Exile" has efficient translations of Guillen, Alberti, Lorca, Machado and others.

In this series Ferlinghetti's "Pictures of the Gone World" offers his own poetry in a flowing variety of open-running lines. He develops a personal, ritual anecdote as a fresh type of recognition, with acute visual perceptions. He seems to have learned something from James Laughlin. His work measures a racy young maturity of experience.

Most of the young poets have not yet published books, but two others who have should be mentioned. They are: James Harmon and Paul Dreykus. Harmon's "In Praise of Eponymous Iahu" (Bern Porter) is struggling between a traditional, mellifluous type of lyric like "Song" and realistic poetry in the manner of "Hawk Inlet." "Stone and Pulse," by Dreykus (Porpoise Book Shop) has esthetic poems like "Light on Two Canvases," about Miro, and a realistic one, "For Observation," about "An angerfleshed man."

OF the still bookless poets, Philip Whalen has somewhat Poundian poems and a highly successful refrain "Love You" in a direct and forceful poem entitled "3 Variations: All About Love." Gary Snyder's poetry is most like Rexroth's, not due so much to direct influence as to identity of sources. Both owe much to Far Eastern verse and philosophy, both are deeply bound into the natural world of stars, birds, mountains and flowers. Michael McClure writes with grace and charm on "For the Death of 100 Whales" and "Point Lobos: Animism," striving for "The rising, the exuberance, when the mystery is unveiled."

Surrounding this young Bay region group are older poets like Josephine Miles, Yvor Winters, Robert Horan, James Schevill (whose verse drama about Roger Williams was recently produced in Providence), Anthony Ostroff, Leonard Wolf, Thomas Parkinson, Albert Cook and others.

The young group is marked naturally by volatility. It seems to be a group today, but nobody knows whether it will survive as a group and make a mark on the national poetic consciousness. Poetry being a highly individualistic expression of mind, soul and personality, it would seem that the idea of a group at all is a misnaming. It may be so. These poets all differ one from another. It may be that one or more individualists will survive the current group manifestation.

It is certain that there is a new, vital group consciousness now among young poets in the Bay region. However unpublished they may be, many of these young poets have a numerous and enthusiastic audience. They acquire this audience by their own efforts. Through their many readings they have in some cases a larger audience than more cautiously presented poets in the East.

They are finely alive, they believe something new can be done with the art of poetry, they are hostile to gloomy critics, and the reader is invited to look into and enjoy their work as it appears. They have exuberance and a young will to kick down the doors of older consciousness and established practice in favor of what they think is vital and new.

This first edition of *To Eberhart from Ginsberg* was printed & published by Michael McCurdy at the Penmaen Press in Lincoln, Massachusetts, and completed in March, 1976. Of an edition of 1500, 300 were hardbound, numbered and signed by Richard Eberhart and Allen Ginsberg. "West Coast Rhythms" was published originally by *The New York Times Book Review* in September, 1956.

Typographic design is by Michael McCurdy. The Times New Roman type was set by Michael Bixler, and the paper is Warren's Olde Style. Robert Burlen & Son bound both hard and soft editions and Robert Hauser created the binding design for the hardcover edition. Jerome Kaplan's relief etchings were printed directly from the original plates. Editorial assistance was provided by Deborah McCurdy.

This is number   .